NLAN

RIPPLES

Patricia Scanlan is the author of ten Number
One best-selling novels, *City Girl*, *Apartment
3B*, *Finishing Touches*, *City Woman*, *Foreign
Affairs*, *Mirror Mirror*, *Promises Promises*, *City
Lives*, *Francesca's Party* and *Two for Joy*. She
has published three adult literacy books:
Second Chance, *Ripples* and *Fair-Weather
Friend*. She lives in Dubl'

NEW ISLAND *Open Door*

RIPPLES
First published 1999
by New Island
2 Brookside
Dundrum Road
Dublin 14

www.newisland.ie

A CIP catalogue record for this book is available from the British Library

ISBN 1 902602 13 7

New Island receives financial assistance from
The Arts Council (An Chomhairle Ealaíon), Dublin, Ireland.

Typeset by New Island
Printed in Ireland by ColourBooks
Cover design by Artmark

Distributed By:
Grass Roots Press
Toll Free: 1-888-303-3213
Fax: (780) 413-6582
Web Site: www.grassrootsbooks.net

Dear Reader,

On behalf of myself and the other contributing authors, I would like to welcome you to the first Open Door series. We hope that you enjoy the books and that reading becomes a lasting pleasure in your life.

Warmest wishes,

Patricia Scanlan.

Patricia Scanlan
Series Editor

THE OPEN DOOR SERIES IS DEVELOPED WITH THE ASSISTANCE OF THE CITY OF DUBLIN VOCATIONAL EDUCATION COMMITTEE.

Chapter One

"You're a stupid cow. That's what you are!"

"And you're a mean bastard. I wish you'd get the hell out of here and never come back."

"Maybe I will. You big mouth – "

Ciara McHugh pressed her thumbs into her ears. They were at it again. Shouting and roaring. Ranting and raving. She hated them. Why couldn't they be like other parents? Why did they have to be fighting all the time?

Why couldn't her mother leave her

dad alone? She was always nagging him.

Nag, nag, nag.

He'd just ignore her. That would make Alison worse and she'd say something to get him going. Then they'd be yelling and shouting at each other.

Her dad's face would go dark with temper. Ciara was often afraid that he'd hit her mother. Sometimes she'd lie on her bed and her heart would pound so loudly she'd feel it was going to burst out of her chest.

Ciara heard the door slam. Hard. It seemed to shake the whole house. She heard the engine of the car start. That would be her dad. He'd drive off after a row and not come home for hours.

There was a dull silence in the house. Soon her mother would come upstairs to Ciara's room. She'd start giving out about Barry, telling Ciara that Barry was selfish and cruel. She'd say that he'd never given her any support in their marriage. He wasn't like their best friend Mike.

Alison thought Mike was a great husband and father.

She was always saying, "See how Mike helps around the house. He cooks dinners at the weekend, instead of sitting with his nose stuck into a football match on TV.

"See how Mike helps his kids with their homework.

"See how Mike takes them out at weekends and gives them … *quality* time."

Alison always paused before she said "quality time". She made it sound like something holy and reverent. She was always reading books about relationships and quality time and communication.

"Mike … *communicates* … with his kids. Your father can't *communicate*, Ciara. I've spent years, *years*, trying to get him to talk to me. Trying to get him to share our life, the way Mike and Kathy share theirs. It's like banging my head off a stone wall."

Her mother always rolled her eyes dramatically at that part.

"I tell you, Ciara, if I can make a go of it with someone else, I bloody well will! I'm not wasting any more time on that thick, squinty-eyed shit. Life's not a *rehearsal*, Ciara. We only get one chance on the merry-go-round. Always remember that. And if you've any sense – *never* get married. You don't want to end up like me. Stuck with a selfish, cruel, heartless bastard." Alison usually burst into tears at that point.

When her mother threatened to go off with someone else, it always frightened Ciara. She didn't know what would happen to her if her parents split up. Where would her daddy go? Ciara's stomach tightened. It always did when she thought about it. Butterflies danced up and down. A tear rolled down her cheek. She felt very scared.

Chapter Two

Ciara didn't think her dad was that bad.

He didn't drink. That was good. Liz Kelly's father was always drunk. Once, he'd even puked up his dinner in front of a gang of them who were staying over for a slumber party. Poor Liz was so embarrassed. She burst into tears and ran up to her room.

Ciara's dad was good for giving lifts, even though he moaned about it. When his football team won and he was in a good humour, he sometimes even gave her a pound.

His team were doing very badly this season. Financially, it had been a bit of a disaster for her, Ciara thought glumly. She scribbled on the brown paper cover of her copy. She could do with some extra money. She'd been invited to another slumber party in a friend's house, and she'd have to bring a present.

It was going to be mixed.

Alison said it was OK to go. She told her not to say anything to Barry. Alison felt that Barry was far too strict. She wanted Ciara to be independent. To stand on her own two feet.

It was going to be a camping slumber party. They were going to buy some of that new alcoholic lemonade and get langered.

Ciara had tasted it once at Sharon Ryan's barbecue in August. It had made her feel nice and woozy. She'd smoked three fags as well. She didn't really like smoking, but it was a cool thing to do. She wanted to be part of the gang.

She was the youngest in the gang. Twelve. The only one not in secondary school.

Ciara sighed deeply. She'd be starting secondary school next year. She'd have to do her assessment in February, and she was very worried about it.

Her maths were a disaster. She hated them.

Sara Stuart was dead lucky. Her dad was a wizard at maths. He was great for helping her. Mike Stuart was a really nice dad, even if he was a bit strict, Ciara thought enviously. Sara wasn't allowed to go to the slumber party. She was freaking out about it. Sara was her best friend.

Secretly, deep down, Ciara didn't

actually want to go to the slumber party. Declan Mooney was going to be at it. Ciara didn't like him any more. Once she'd thought she fancied him, but he'd given her a French kiss. She'd thought it was *disgusting*! He'd also touched her up once, and that had made her feel dirty.

Yuck! Ciara shuddered.

She wished that she could stay at home. But her dad was going to a match and her mother had arranged to go dancing in Tomangos when she knew Ciara was going on a sleep-over. Her mother was always going to Tomangos.

Why, why, why couldn't she have normal parents like the Stuarts? Kathy Stuart wouldn't be caught dead in Tomangos. She was a *real* mother. She baked bread and tarts and cakes. She made proper dinners. Not burgers and chips, Alison's idea of a dinner, Ciara thought angrily.

She heard her mother coming upstairs. She didn't want to get an ear-bashing about the row she'd overheard between her parents. Ciara jumped up. She switched off the light and dived under the duvet, still in her clothes. She heard Alison open the door and peer in cautiously.

"Are you awake, lovie?"

Leave me alone. Leave me alone. Leave me alone, Ciara screamed silently. She lay perfectly still, eyes scrunched tightly shut.

"Ciara?" Alison tried again, hopefully.

Ciara knew that her mother needed a shoulder to cry on.

She always did after a row. It wasn't fair! It was very confusing. She felt guilty. Maybe she should comfort her mother. She was just about to sit up when Alison closed the door with a little sigh.

Ciara lay in the dark and let tears brim from her eyes into a hot, wet waterfall down her cheeks. Her stomach felt tied up in knots again. She felt sick.

She couldn't do her maths. She didn't want to go to the slumber party. Her parents were fighting. Life was horrible. She wondered again what would happen to her if her parents split up, or worse still, got a divorce. She didn't want this to happen. She just wanted them to be normal.

Chapter Three

Brenda Johnson smiled happily as she lay back in her lover's arms. She hadn't been expecting Barry to call tonight. He'd arrived unexpectedly just after nine. She'd been watching the news. It was all about the passing of the amendment for divorce.

The YES vote had won by a very small majority. The relief she'd felt had been enormous. Then the terrible fear when some senator and his supporters had argued the decision.

Brenda wanted to strangle him with

her bare hands. Didn't the fool realise that this was her last chance? And the last chance for many like her.

She and Barry had been having an affair for the past three years. She knew Alison suspected. But Alison wasn't bothered by it. How many times had her best friend said, 'You can have him. I'm sick of him.'

The trouble with Alison was that she didn't appreciate Barry. She'd never looked after him. Not the way Brenda did. The rows between Barry and Alison had started when Ciara was born. That's what Alison said. She said that Barry hated not being the centre of attention.

Maybe it was true, Brenda agreed.

She'd known Barry as long as Alison had. Barry *did* like being the centre of attention. Not in a flashy, in-your-face way. His way was much more crafty.

He'd sit, shoulders hunched up, staring out from behind his glasses with his Poor-Sad-Misunderstood-Me-With-the-Weight-of-the-World-on-My-Shoulders look.

You had to feel sorry for him. You'd ask him what was wrong. He'd say "Nothing." And then you'd have to keep at him. Wrinkling it out bit by bit.

You'd get moans about the pressure he was under at work. Or about Alison and the state she'd left the house in. Once he'd said to her, "Look, Brenda, I'm a loner. I always have been and I always will be. Don't even try and understand me." He'd been feeling very sorry for himself that night.

But of course she understood him. She understood him more than anyone. She loved him very much. And if he'd let her, she'd make him happy. Much happier than Alison had ever made him.

It was just that Brenda was never quite sure where she stood with him.

He swore that he loved her. He wanted to be with her, he said. His marriage to Alison was over. They were just staying together for Ciara's sake. He promised that when Ciara was finished college in another ten years he and Brenda would be together for good. He had his responsibilities as a parent. He knew she understood.

It was very decent of him to be so concerned for his daughter, Brenda thought stoutly. He was a good, sound, honest, hard-working man. She couldn't fault him for taking his responsibilities so seriously. That was a good trait surely? But ten years seemed like such a long time away.

She'd be over *fifty*.

Crikey! What an awful thought.

Brenda quickly put it to the back of her mind.

She stroked Barry's back. He had pale, pasty, spotty skin. Barry wasn't God's gift in the looks department, or even in the sex department, come to think of it. But beggars couldn't be choosers. He was her last chance to have a man of her own.

Her bubble of happiness at his unexpected arrival was getting a little flat. Imagine even thinking like that! Was this how pathetic she'd become?

Chapter Four

Why couldn't she have been like all the rest of her friends? Brenda thought sadly. Why couldn't she have met a nice man? A man who would have courted her properly. Brought her flowers and chocolates. Held car doors open for her. A man who would have proposed and given her a ring and a day to remember.

A wedding day with a beautiful white dress and veil and all the trimmings.

Had it been so much to ask for? Had she just grasped at Barry because the years were slipping by? Because she'd been so panicky and lonely. Afraid of ending up a spinster on the shelf. With no man to show for a lifetime of Friday and Saturday nights dolling herself up to go out on the hunt to find a mate?

Year after year. Dance after dance. Disco after disco. Night club after night club.

Was she crazy to believe that Barry would divorce Alison and marry her?

How happy she'd been to vote YES to divorce.

She could still remember how firmly she'd marked the X with the black pencil in the polling booth. She'd been so happy to hear the news this evening that the law was to be passed in favour of divorce. She was sure Barry would have been pleased too. When she said it to him, he'd just grunted and said, "One marriage was enough for me."

They could live together. It was much less complicated, he muttered.

Of course, she'd agreed. But deep, deep down she was scared. She wanted him to *want* to marry her. That was how it should be. What if he dumped her for some babe in the office? If he could cheat on Alison, he could cheat on her. The thought came out of the blue. She buried it.

She wasn't going to think about that now. He was here, in her arms. That was all that mattered.

He wouldn't have been here if there hadn't been a row. Another sneaky, horrible little thought escaped.

What was wrong with her, for crying out loud? Another even more awful thought came to torment her. Maybe she was starting the change of life early. Hell! That was all she needed. To become a dried-up old prune as well.

She thought of Eileen O'Neill at work. Eileen was having an affair with a married man. He had four kids. His wife knew about it. He spent Friday to Monday with Eileen and the other three days at home.

Eileen was nuts about him. She was so cracked about him she'd even got in Sky Sports so that he and his pals could watch live football. He'd promised Eileen many times that he'd marry her if he could. Safe in the knowledge that divorce wasn't legal in Ireland.

Well it looked as if it was going to become legal now. It would be interesting to see if he kept his word. He was an out-and-out bastard though. Not satisfied with one mistress, he had several strings to his bow. He didn't think being faithful to Eileen was important. But still she took him back and listened to his lies, and believed him when he told her his flings were over. On two occasions he'd been unfaithful to her, but she'd just closed her eyes to it.

Brenda snorted. What a foolish woman she was. There he was, living with his wife, living with his mistress, seeing other women. Having his cake and eating it. And Eileen was so desperate to keep the lying, cheating, two-faced creep, she'd got Sky Sports for him!

Never! Never in a million years would Brenda sink to such levels. She had her pride. Besides Barry wasn't *anything* like that two-faced rat of Eileen's. Barry had *integrity*.

Brenda felt a little happier. He'd change his mind about the divorce. She was sure of it. If only Alison would find a new man. That would solve everything, Brenda thought with renewed hope. Maybe it would happen soon. In a few days' time, Alison was going to Tomangos with some friends. Ciara was going to a party. Brenda was going to have Barry all to herself for a few hours. They would go to a football match together. She wanted to share every part of his life.

"I suppose I'd better go home," she heard her lover say.

How she longed for the time when he could stay all night. That would be the most wonderful thing in the world.

Chapter Five

Lillian McHugh snuggled under the quilt and pulled it up over her ears. The bed was lovely and warm. She could hear the rain lashing against the window. *I think I'll have a lazy day today*, she decided.

Lillian smiled. How lovely! Who would have ever thought that she'd be able to lie in bed and do exactly what she liked. She could stay in bed all day if she wanted to. At seventy years of age, she was a liberated woman!

Thank you, God, for making me a widow.

It was a heart-felt prayer. Since her husband Tom had died two years ago, her life had changed completely. She'd discovered a whole new world.

She didn't have to get up at the crack of dawn any more to cook a breakfast for a cross, grumpy old man. She didn't have to wash smelly socks. She didn't have to iron shirts. There were a lot of things she didn't have to do any more.

Lillian had hated Tom McHugh, her dead husband. They'd been married for forty-five years. He'd made her life a misery. She'd had to put up with his moods. His meanness. And his bad temper. Tom had been a most selfish man.

He'd courted her for three years, and then married her. She, like a fool, had believed that life would be happy-ever-after. She'd mistaken his quiet, reserved ways for shyness. The relief of having a ring on her finger had been wonderful. She wouldn't end up an old maid! The excitement of having a home of her own had helped her overlook her disappointment in her new husband.

She'd thought that they would do things together. Go to the cinema, the theatre. Or even go out for a meal now and again. But once the honeymoon was over and they'd started living in the small terraced house they'd bought in Fairview, her dreams had quickly turned to ashes.

Tom wasn't the slightest bit interested in them doing anything together. He went to work. Read his sports news in the paper. On Friday he went to his football matches.

He expected his breakfast on the table at seven a.m. sharp. His dinner had to be on the table when he came home from work in the evening. They had sex every Saturday night and that was over almost before it started. After a few grunts and groans and rough fumblings Tom would roll over and fall asleep.

That had been the pattern throughout their marriage.

They'd had one child. Barry. He was a quiet, lonely boy. He'd left home as soon as he'd done his Leaving Cert and gone to live in a flat in Drumcondra.

Barry had married a girl from Phibsboro. Alison. They had one child. A little girl, Ciara. Lillian didn't see much of them. They had rarely come to visit when Tom was alive. Christmas, Easter, that was it. Lillian couldn't blame them. Who'd want to come and try and make conversation with the old grump sitting by the fire?

Well, Tom was dead and she was glad of it. She was in an active retirement group now. She went bowling. She went flower-arranging. And they were always going on little trips to places of interest.

Lillian was having the time of her life. She was going to make the most of it, for as long as she could.

But today it was raining. The weather had changed and she was staying in bed. Lillian picked up her library book. A steamy romance. She curled up for a long read.

Life was good.

Chapter Six

"The McHugh's were a bit frosty tonight," Mike Stuart said.

"That's an understatement if ever I heard one," his wife, Kathy, murmured out of the side of her mouth. "They'd have been at home in the Arctic. They had a big row earlier in the week, Alison said."

"What's new?" Mike asked glumly.

They stood at the front door waving goodbye to their guests. They were caught in the wide beam of the car's headlights as Barry McHugh reversed down the drive. He gave a toot on his horn. Beside him, his wife Alison looked fed up.

Kathy knew that the tight smile she gave them would be gone in seconds after the car headed towards the main road. She gave a sigh of relief as the Lancer's rear lights disappeared into the night.

Tonight had been a disaster! Alison had sniped at Barry constantly. At times he'd ignored her completely. This had been like a red rag to a bull. Several glasses of wine hadn't helped. As Alison's rage and resentment overflowed, she'd turned to her friends and said angrily, "I'm married to the biggest bastard you could meet."

"Either take your go now, Alison, or lose it. You've been holding up the game for the last five minutes," Barry said coldly. His eyes were like flints behind his glasses. He glared at her.

"Get lost! I'll go when I'm ready. Just because you think you're *Mister Intelligence*. Well you're not. You're just a cheat. Who else would try and get away with putting Monaco down? And then say it was a *font*. It's not in the dictionary. It shouldn't be allowed. And you shouldn't get a triple word score."

"Well if you weren't so *thick*, you'd know that it was a font. I'll show it to you on the computer when we get home."

"Oh, stick your bloody computer. You should have married one, you spend so much time on that one in the office," Alison snapped.

She slapped down her letters.

"Is that the best you can do? *Rat!* Pathetic!" Barry's brown eyes flashed with scorn.

"Well I'm married to one, aren't I?" Alison retorted coldly. "Don't forget it's a double word score."

"The first one you've managed so far," Barry jeered as he wrote down the score.

They'd been playing their usual Saturday-night game of Scrabble. A tradition that went back to the carefree giddy days of their early twenties. They'd all been newly-weds. The future had looked rosy. Now, fourteen years later, things weren't looking too rosy for Barry and Alison. Much to Mike and Kathy's dismay.

Over the last few months things had become very bad. The weekly game of Scrabble that they'd always looked forward to, with a few drinks and a Chinese take-away, was becoming an ordeal.

"I've never seen them as bad as they

were tonight," Kathy said. She collected the dirty glasses. Then she emptied the cold, greasy remains of the Chinese take-away into the bin.

"Why they ever married each other I'll never know. They're like chalk and cheese. They always were. I mean Alison is always gadding about. And Barry hates going anywhere," Mike said as he picked the bones of a cold spare rib.

"Put that in the bin, you glutton." Kathy made a face. "They say opposites attract. Maybe it worked at the start but it's not working now."

"Yes, well, Alison made the big mistake of thinking that she was going to change Barry. He'll never change. He's not even making an effort now. I don't think that he wants to come over to us on Saturday night any more. All he wants to do is go to his football matches. Or bury himself in his work. He lives in that office."

"Would you say that Barry's got another woman?" Kathy asked her husband. She had often thought there had to be someone else. "He can't be spending all those nights at work."

"Barry! Barry McHugh! Don't be *daft*, woman," Mike scoffed.

He licked his fingers. "He'd run a mile if a woman came near him. Imagine Barry sitting down and having a conversation with a woman. It's hard enough for him to have a conversation with us. And he's known us for years."

"Maybe you're right." Kathy poured Fairy Liquid into a basin of hot water. "He's great fun, though, when he's in form. He's got a good sense of humour. I feel sorry for him sometimes. Alison is always nagging him.

"Barry likes being nagged. He likes

being told what to do. He never makes decisions. Alison makes them all. Did you hear her telling him that he was to get his hair cut next week? And telling him that she'd told Brenda Johnson that he'd tile her bathroom. Without even *asking* him! What is he, a man or a mouse?"

Mike picked up the towel and started to dry the dishes.

"It's like he's the child and she's the mother. It's always been like that with them. That would drive me nuts. If I came home and found out that you'd told Brenda Johnson that I'd tile her bathroom, you know what your answer would be." He grinned.

"Alison was always a bossy boots. I wouldn't inflict Poison-Dwarf Johnson on you. I'd know better." Kathy giggled.

Brenda Johnson was Alison

McHugh's best friend. Kathy didn't like her. She thought she was sly. She was always flirting with other women's husbands. Brenda was unmarried. She was in her early forties. She had recently bought a house that needed a lot of renovation. Brenda was an expert at the Poor-Little-Me-I'm-a-Helpless-Female act. Every man she knew was being roped in to help decorate. Barry was doing the lion's share.

"*Poison Dwarf!* Miaow! Brenda's not in the good books. What has she done now?"

"She had the nerve to say that I didn't know what stress was. She said that I had you to provide for me. She said that I could come and go as I pleased because I'm a housewife. She thinks that I have very little to do," Kathy said crossly.

"Well I do provide for you. You can

come and go as you please," Mike said innocently.

"You know what I mean." Kathy flicked frothy suds at her husband. He flicked back and drenched her.

"Stop it," she squealed.

"Shush, you'll wake the kids," Mike warned.

"Well if the baby wakes up *you* won't be getting any nookey tonight. It's your turn to get up to her. And *I* intend sleeping my brains out. In the spare room if necessary," Kathy said smugly.

"We'll see about that." Mike dropped the towel. He grabbed his wife and gave her a long smoochy kiss.

"Let's leave the rest of the washing up and the *two* of us can sleep in the spare room." He nuzzled her ear.

Kathy laughed. Even after ten years of marriage and three children, Mike still turned her on. She loved him passionately. Hand in hand they crept upstairs into the spare bedroom.

Chapter Seven

Later, snuggled in the curve of Mike's arm, Kathy said sleepily, "I mean it, Mike. Would you say that Barry and Brenda are having a fling?"

"*Who* in their right mind would want to have an affair with Bug-Eyes Johnson? Are you *mad*? She wouldn't shut up long enough to let someone kiss her. She loves the sound of her own voice too much. She's such a bloody know-all. Who would want to listen to that squeaky little voice of hers? Day in, day out. What man would want to watch her flicking that lank, greasy brown hair of hers over her shoulders the way she does?"

"Well, Barry didn't say that he *wouldn't* tile her bathroom for her," Kathy pointed out. "He's always doing bits and pieces for her. Maybe *he* likes her. Alison's always telling her that she can have him. Big joke! I think Brenda thinks that she's serious."

"She's bossy enough for him anyway. She's even more of a dictator than Alison." Mike yawned.

"Ah, Alison's not that bad," Kathy defended her friend. "If she didn't nag Barry he'd never do anything except watch soccer and play with his computers."

"If I lived in their house that's all I'd want to do. It's like a pigsty. Alison is no good at house-keeping. *You* don't know how lucky you are. I never watch soccer. I don't have a computer," Mike murmured into her hair.

"And I don't have a job, like Alison. I'm always here to cook your dinner. I light the fire. I have your shirts ironed every morning. You don't know how lucky you are, buster !"

"I know how lucky I am," Mike whispered. His arms tightening around her.

"Poor Barry and Alison. It's horrible, isn't it?" Kathy said sadly.

"I couldn't stick a marriage like that. All that bitterness and anger and resentment. It's almost as if they hate each other now. Maybe they'd be better off divorced," Mike declared.

"Oh don't say that, Mike," Kathy exclaimed.

"Well it's true. What kind of a life have they got now? No life. The trouble with Alison and Barry is that they are both very selfish people. There's very little give-and-take. Barry should never have got married. He should never have had a child either. He's not prepared to make the effort. Poor Ciara's a nuisance to him. He thinks that once he provides financially for her that his responsibility is over. He's not prepared to give any more." He stroked Kathy's hair.

"It's like our friendship. If we didn't have them over and keep in touch he wouldn't bother. It's too much effort. He's a strange chap."

"I wonder does our friendship mean anything to him? Or is it just habit?" Kathy asked.

"You never know with Barry. You never know what's really in his mind. Barry is very calculating. He always was. He says nothing much, but takes it all in. At the end of the day he always puts himself first."

"He's very good-natured though. He'd never see you stuck. Maybe it's just a bad patch. Maybe they'll work things out." Kathy sighed.

"I hope so, because if they don't, I don't really want to go away for a long weekend with them. I don't want to have to sit listening to rows for three days."

"Me neither," Kathy agreed glumly. "But I've always looked forward to that weekend away without the kids. It wouldn't be the same going on our own. Remember the time we went to West Cork? We found out that the hotel was an out-and-out kip. Then Barry told the mad one behind the desk that he was from Bord Failte. There was no way that he and his party were going to spend one minute there. Let alone a night. And he waved his union card under her nose and she believed him and gave him back the deposit. God, we legged it out of there so fast.

"Remember the time we were camping and Alison set the tent on fire?" Kathy laughed.

"Yes, and remember the time we went on the Shannon cruiser and Barry caught a pike and chased you along the quay wall and you tripped over a rope?"

"I nearly broke my neck." Kathy grinned in the dark at the memory. "We had fun though, didn't we?"

"Ah maybe they'll get over it. Maybe a weekend away would do them all the good in the world," Mike, declared sleepily. He always looked on the bright side.

"Maybe," Kathy agreed. But she wondered if they'd ever have such good times together again. The way things were going, it didn't look like it.

Alison had told her in the kitchen that she'd got off with a fella she'd met at a dance. She'd enjoyed a mighty good snog with him too. If she met someone else, she was off. Barry could like it or lump it.

That didn't sound like someone who was prepared to try and make a go of things. Poor little Ciara. Kathy's motherly heart went out to her god-daughter. She felt very angry.

Couldn't either of them see what they were doing to the child? Couldn't they see how insecure she was? That they were always fighting in front of her? Mike was right, they were bloody selfish. Neither of them was taking any responsibility for what they were doing to their daughter.

Kathy didn't like the crowd that

Ciara hung out with. Imagine letting a twelve-year-old go to a mixed slumber party!

Sara, Kathy and Mike's daughter, had been asked also. She was in a mega-huff with her parents because she wasn't allowed to go. She could stay in her huff. No way was she going to any mixed slumber parties.

It was very difficult though. Ciara was allowed to do so much. In Sara's eyes, Mike and Kathy were much too strict. It was starting to cause terrible hassle.

Kathy sighed. Bringing up kids was no joke. Where did you draw the line? You had to start letting go sometime. But you had to protect them too. At least she and Mike were trying. Barry and Alison didn't seem to have any such worries.

But then Ciara was very "responsible"

for her age, according to Alison. That was what she'd said when Kathy had asked her why she'd agreed to let Ciara go to the slumber party. It suited Alison to think that. It let her off the hook when hard decisions had to be made.

"Responsible" was not the way Kathy would describe Barry and Alison right now, she thought crossly. She gave Mike a dig in the ribs to stop him snoring, before drifting off to sleep herself.

Chapter Eight

Ciara felt sick.

One of the fellas had brought vodka, in a Seven-Up bottle, to the party. She'd drank some. It had made her feel very odd. Then she'd smoked a cigarette. That had made her feel dizzy.

The music was very loud. She didn't really like Oasis. She much preferred the Spice Girls. Her friend's parents had gone off to the pub and two fellas that hadn't been invited had gate-crashed. They were causing trouble.

Ciara wanted to go home.

Declan Mooney grabbed her.

"Let's snog," he said.

"In your dreams," Ciara answered back, snootily. She hoped he'd get the message. Declan ignored her and kissed her anyway. She thought she was going to puke.

"Can't wait to see you in your nightie. Whose tent are you sleeping in?" he asked hopefully.

"Not yours, for sure. Besides you know it's one tent for the boys and one for the girls," Ciara snapped.

Declan winked.

"We're coming visiting."

"Get lost," Ciara slurred crossly. She didn't want to sleep in a tent. She wanted to be safe and snug in her own bed, knowing that Declan Mooney couldn't get near her.

She felt funny. Her fingers closed around her house key in her jeans pocket. She always carried a key. She got home from school at three, every day. Alison was never home from work until after six. Sometimes later.

Ciara was used to being on her own in the house. She wouldn't mind being alone until her dad came home from his match tonight.

Ciara slipped out the side gate. She hurried along the footpath. Every now and then she turned around to see if anyone had seen her. She felt very sick and dizzy. Her knees started to shake. She felt scared as she hunkered down, trying to take deep breaths.

Next thing, she heard the worried voice of Mike Stuart. "Ciara, Ciara, are you all right?"

"I drank some stuff. I feel funny."

"Come on. Come home with me." Mike sounded very kind. He helped her up. Ciara leaned against him.

His house was just across the street.

It was a huge relief to sink down onto his sofa and close her eyes.

She had never felt so sick in her life.

Chapter Nine

Mike was furious. "It's a bloody disgrace! Those kids are all half-pissed down in Hennessys'. I rang some of the parents. How could Barry and Alison let Ciara go to something like that? They should be shot."

Kathy was also raging. "They don't care about that poor child. Do you know that they left her on her own in the house after school with two men who were fitting a new alarm system? Maybe they were perfectly nice men. But who's to know these days? Have they no sense? I wouldn't leave Sara on her own with two strangers for three minutes, let alone three hours. It's just not safe any more. Have those two lost their marbles? Have they any sense of responsibility? By God I'm going to give Barry and Alison an earful when I bring Ciara home. She's out gadding. He's out at his match. That poor child is wandering the streets pissed out of her skull. Haven't they a great life all the same, the pair of them?" Kathy's lips tightened.

"Let her stay the night," Mike suggested.

"No, Mike. I want Barry to see Ciara's little white face, God love her. I'll being her home in an hour or so. Anyway she wants to go home to her own bed."

"OK, maybe you're right," Mike agreed.

★

An hour later Kathy drove her tired goddaughter home. She'd tried phoning to check that Barry was there. The phone was engaged. So one of them must be there, thought Kathy.

She felt terribly sorry for Ciara.

It was time that Barry and Alison accepted some responsibility for their child. She was going to tell them so.

Barry's car was in the drive. There was a light on in the hall.

"I've got my key. The bell's not working properly. You can't hear it if the TV's on," Ciara said.

She was scared. "Dad's going to kill me."

"No he won't. I'll explain. I know you won't drink again after this," Kathy said kindly.

"I promise I won't. Honest," Ciara said earnestly. She slid the key into the lock.

Kathy followed her into the sitting-room. She heard Ciara gasp in horror before she laid eyes on the sight that sent Ciara running from the room, crying loudly.

Barry cursed.

Brenda squeaked, "Oh my God!" as she lay underneath him on the sofa.

Both of them were naked.

"I … I … " Kathy stuttered. "I'll bring Ciara home with me."

I knew it, she thought. I knew he was having an affair with Brenda. Mike couldn't see past the end of his nose! She had to get out of here. This was a nightmare.

"Blast you, Barry! Could you not have gone to that one's house?" Kathy exploded

She hurried upstairs after Ciara

"Come on, love. Come and stay the night with me."

"I hate him. I hate him. I hate all of them."

"I know, pet, we'll talk about it at

home. Come on, you need a good night's sleep."

Kathy's heart bled for her. Ciara, only five weeks older then her own Sara, had just had her innocence and security snatched from her in a very cruel way.

Kathy had lost all respect for Barry. Having an affair was his business. But couldn't he have had the decency to conduct it somewhere other than his own home.

Brenda was supposed to be Alison's best friend. Some friend. She'd always had a thing for Barry. Even before he was married. But then Alison had told her she could have him. She was out on the man-hunt too.

It was crazy. The McHugh's marriage was well-and-truly over. That was for sure.

Kathy felt really sad. She led the

weeping young girl out to the car. Hard as the break-up was for Barry and Alison, it was a thousand times worse for Ciara.

Chapter Ten

Ciara lay in bed shivering. She couldn't get warm.

Sara, her best friend, was asleep on a pump-up bed on the floor.

Sara had been very kind. She'd given Ciara her bed. She'd put her arms around her and told her that everything would be all right. Kathy and Mike had said so too.

Ciara desperately wanted to believe them. But now they were all asleep. She wished she could sleep. All she wanted to do was forget the awful thing that had happened.

Maybe it was a nightmare. She might wake up and discover that she had dreamt it all.

Ciara took a deep breath.

She gave herself a pinch.

It hurt.

She wasn't asleep having a dream. It had all happened. She had seen her dad and Brenda bonking on the sofa. It was horrible.

What would her mam say when she found out?

Ciara knew the answer to that.

Alison wouldn't care. She was out dancing in Tomangos. Maybe she was with another man. She always said if a chance came her way, she'd take it.

Why did they have to be like that? Why couldn't they be normal parents? Why couldn't they love each other and be happy? Like the Stuarts. Why did they have to ruin her life?

Ciara cried in the dark. Big sobs that nearly choked her. She was afraid she would wake Sara. But Sara slept on, snoring gently.

What was going to happen now?

Her dad would leave. She just knew that. He was always saying that he was leaving.

Ciara cried even harder. She loved her dad. Even if he was moody. She didn't want him to move out of the house. She always felt safe when he was there. She liked knowing that he was downstairs watching his sport while she was up in her room. She'd hear him cheering and yelling when his team scored a goal. That always made Ciara feel good. She knew then that her father was happy for a little while. She liked to see her father happy.

Maybe it was all her fault. If she'd been a boy all this might never have happened. Men wanted sons, didn't they? Barry could have taken a son to football matches. He never took her to a football match. He never took her anywhere. Now he probably never would. He'd leave home and forget all about her.

Ciara sobbed her heart out, hoping against hope that Sara would wake up and talk to her. And tell her that everything would be all right.

Sara slept on.

Chapter Eleven

One year later ...

Thank God he was staying with his fancy woman tonight.

Lillian McHugh gave a big sigh of relief as she plonked herself in front of the TV. She was having a cheese and tomato sandwich with a cup of coffee. She always liked to get the midday news and weather and then watch her daily TV show on RTÉ One.

Barry wasn't coming home for lunch. She could watch *Twelve to One* in peace without having to worry about cooking him a meal. She smiled at her favourite presenters, Marty and Ciana, as they read out the line-up for the programme before the news. What a lovely couple. Nice, pleasant people.

She wouldn't mind cooking a meal for Marty Whelan. He's a lovely twinkle in his eye. He wasn't a bit like Barry with his scowls and bad humours.

What had she done to deserve this trial in her life? Lillian wondered angrily.

It was almost eight months since Barry had arrived on her doorstep. He'd muttered that there was a bit of trouble at home. Could he stay with her for a while, he'd asked.

Lillian had been dumbstruck. What could she say? She couldn't turn her own son away, even though he was the last person in the world that she wanted living with her.

It was a terrible thing to admit to. The truth was she didn't much like her son. Her only child.

He was so like his father.

Grumpy. Bad-tempered.

He'd moved in, bag and baggage. Up to the front bedroom.

The days turned into weeks. Then months. Slowly but surely her precious, hard-won freedom slipped away.

She washed and ironed his clothes. Made his bed. Cooked his meals for him. She couldn't even watch the programmes she liked on TV any more if there was sport on.

He had another girlfriend. He'd told her that at the start. He usually spent the weekends with her. Lillian looked forward so much to those weekends. They kept her sane.

But if Barry and the girlfriend had a

row, which they often did, he ended up staying with Lillian. She bitterly resented the situation. She just couldn't bring herself to ask him to leave. She'd never been good at standing up for herself. A lifetime married to Tom McHugh had seen to that. Now it was as if he'd come back to haunt her. Lillian woke up angry in the mornings. She went to bed angry at night.

The midday news came on.

Lillian heard the news reader announce that the first divorce in Ireland was going through the courts. A little flicker of hope glimmered. Maybe Barry would get a divorce and go and marry that Brenda one.

Lillian had never met her, nor did she ever wish to meet her. But if she took Barry off her hands, Lillian would be eternally grateful. She wondered could she pray that Barry would get divorced and remarried. Hardly. It didn't seem right. Praying for your son to get divorced! The church would certainly frown on that.

Maybe she'd just pray that Barry would move out and get a flat on his own. He *surely* didn't want to spend the rest of his life living with her.

It was all so upsetting. Lillian pushed away her untouched sandwich. She wasn't hungry.

The ripples of this marriage break-up were affecting so many lives. Hers and Ciara's most of all. Her life was a hard old grind again. Just like before. And she didn't have the guts to do anything about it. That was the hardest thing of all to live with.

Chapter Twelve

Brenda sat in the staff canteen drinking coffee. The chatter and buzz annoyed her. The rattle of china and cutlery was giving her a headache. She read the headlines.

Once, the news of the first divorce in Ireland going through the courts would have filled her with joy. Now she just didn't know what to think.

Being involved with Barry left her feeling like she was walking on a tightrope. One false move and that was it.

Why wouldn't he commit to her and marry her like she wanted to marry him? Why did he keep using Ciara as an excuse?

It wasn't exactly as if he was Father-of-the-Year-Award material. Actually, he wasn't as good a father as she had once given him credit for.

He admitted it too. But he was too selfish to do anything about it. It was a side of him that Brenda didn't like. She tried not to think about it too often.

If he was living with her permanently, Ciara could spend more time with them. The trouble was, Brenda knew that he was happy enough living with his mother. He was well looked after. Better than when he'd lived with Alison. He had all the home comforts. And he was well fed. Barry liked his food.

He had Brenda for sex when he needed it. Then he could run home to his mammy.

How could she compete with Ma

McHugh? Brenda asked herself over and over.

Barry often told her that his mother liked him living with her. "It makes her feel more secure," he said.

He wouldn't like to "desert" her.

That had chilled Brenda to the bone. Something *drastic* had to be done. She needed to make living with her more attractive to him.

Brenda got up from the table and marched upstairs to her office. She flicked impatiently through the phone book. She knew she couldn't sink any lower. Her pride was in tatters. But needs must, she told herself firmly. She found the number she was looking for and dialled it.

"Hello, I'd like to make an enquiry about getting Sky Sports. How do I go about it?"

Chapter Thirteen

Kathy brushed beaten egg on top of the chicken and mushroom pie and popped it in the oven. It would be cooked by the time the children came in from school. She'd made it specially for Ciara. It was her god-daughter's favourite.

Ciara was spending the weekend with them – yet again.

Kathy frowned.

Alison had phoned with one of her big stories about how she needed Ciara looked after.

She'd told Kathy that she'd got a

lovely offer of a weekend away with her new boyfriend. She couldn't ask Barry and Brenda to take her because it wasn't their weekend to have Ciara. Alison said that they weren't at all flexible about swapping weekend parenting duties.

"And she just loves being with you and Mike. And Sara's her *very* best friend," Alison gushed. As usual.

Kathy was so angry she wanted to tell Barry and Alison *exactly* what she thought of them.

She hadn't seen Barry since that dreadful night when she'd walked in on him and Brenda. That was over a year ago. Since then, he hadn't had the manners to contact her or Mike once. He had never apologised. It was as if they didn't exist in his life.

Some friend he'd turned out to be, not even having the guts to face them.

Or maybe he just didn't want to. He'd dropped them like hot potatoes when he didn't need them. All their happy times together meant nothing. That hurt!

Kathy could accept that Barry couldn't face her, but she couldn't forgive him for the way he was treating Ciara.

She'd never forget Sara telling her last summer that Ciara had got a postcard from her daddy and his girlfriend. They were on holiday. She hoped they'd buy her a nice present.

Barry had only seen Ciara three times last summer. At least Alison had taken her away for a week. Barry had taken his two-weeks' holidays and spent them driving around the country with Brenda.

The best he could do was to send Ciara a postcard. Kathy had been very angry when she'd heard about it.

"It's neglect, Mike. That's what it is. I'm going to have it out with him. And with Alison. The two of them are off having the life of Reilly and it's you and me that are here worrying about Ciara," she raged to her husband.

"And if you cause a row who's going to suffer? Ciara is. Say nothing. It's not our place to interfere. All we can do is be here for Ciara as long as she needs us. If there's an argument they might stop her from seeing us. That poor kid has enough trouble in her life without that. Say nothing," Mike had advised.

Kathy knew he was right. She held her tongue. But it was very hard to stay silent.

Alison was using them at every opportunity. She was always saying how much Ciara loved staying with them. She was trying to make them feel bad if they said that they wouldn't look after her. Kathy was sick of it. Only that she loved Ciara like one of her own, she'd tell them to get lost.

Kathy set the table for dinner. She was most annoyed at the whole set-up. But she could do nothing without hurting Ciara.

That was the worst thing of all.

Chapter Fourteen

Ciara sat in class and listened as her teacher explained the assessment test for getting into secondary school. It was like a huge weight on her shoulders. She was dreading it. She stopped listening. She thought about Robbie Williams instead.

Later, the teacher told the class to take out their maths books. Ciara always felt like a dunce when she tried to do maths. She was going to stay with her friend Sara this weekend. She'd ask Sara's dad to explain Simple Interest to her. Mike was very good at explaining maths.

She was glad to be staying with the Stuarts this weekend. She didn't want to go to Kilkenny with Alison and her new boyfriend. She hated seeing her mother in bed with another man. And she hated seeing her dad in bed with Brenda of the knitting-needle legs.

Ciara bit her nails. They were down to the stubs. They looked awful. No matter how hard she tried to, she couldn't stop biting them.

Biting her nails made her think of food. She hoped Kathy would cook chicken and mushroom pie for the dinner. It always tasted mega.

Everyone thought that she was dead lucky to have a mother like Alison. A mother who let her wear make-up and minis. Who brought her into pubs and gave her sips of wine. And who allowed her have a TV in her room. Her friends thought that Alison, who went to discos and knew all the words of the latest pop songs, was dead cool. Ciara just wished that she'd stay at home and cook real dinners and help her with her home-work. Like Kathy. Kathy was a *proper* mother, Ciara thought enviously. Sara was very lucky.

"Are your ma and da going to get a divorce?" Sadie Flynn whispered. "Someone got a divorce today. It was on the news at lunch time."

"No, they're just separated for a while. They're going to get back together," Ciara whispered back.

She always said that, hoping against hope that it would come true.

"Oh!" said Sadie, disappointed.

The knots tightened in Ciara's stomach. She'd forgotten about the divorce thing. Now it loomed large again.

Her mother and father hated each other. Ciara knew keep down that they would never live together again.

Barry probably wanted to marry Brenda.

Alison probably wanted to marry the new boyfriend.

Ciara didn't like him. He picked his nose. He didn't talk much to her. He drank. It would be awful if he moved into their house.

If her mother and father got a divorce that might happen.

Ciara chewed the top of her pen miserably. Another great worry to add to the ones she had already.

Chapter Fifteen

"*If you wanna be my lover, you gotta get with my friends,*" Alison McHugh sang to herself as she packed her toilet bag for the weekend. She was looking forward to the trip to Kilkenny.

She felt young and carefree. So different from the past few years. It was a joy to be free and almost single again. Alison folded her white, lacy nightdress neatly.

Not that she wanted a divorce. She had given the matter a lot of thought. Alison was happy as she was. She had

the house. She had Ciara. She wasn't
going to disgrace the family name with
a divorce. Brenda could have the rat.
But she wasn't getting her mitts on any
of their money. That would include a
half share of the house and whatever
money that would be divided between
her and Barry if they divorced.

"Tough luck, Brenda. Hands off,"
Alison muttered as she packed her
toothbrush.

Alison didn't want Brenda to
become Mrs McHugh. That would
alter the status between them too
much.

She'd always enjoyed being the
object of Brenda's envy. As long as she
stayed married to Barry, Brenda would
be the poor little spinster who couldn't
quite get a man of her own and had to
settle for used goods.

Alison would have the security of

her wedding ring and still have men attracted to her like moths to a flame. It was almost like being a teenager again.

I'm quite the catch, she thought giddily as she packed her sexy, black suspender belt.

Life had never been so good.

Chapter Sixteen

Barry switched off the news. He slid his Elvis tape into the deck.

So, the first divorce case was going through. No doubt Brenda would give him an ear-bashing tonight. She was as much of a nag as Alison had been.

Women. They were all the same.

Brenda would start about divorce the minute he went in the door. Well, she was barking up the wrong tree there. He'd never promised her marriage. He had no intention of ever getting married again.

Once was enough.

Besides, he was dammed if that cow, Alison, was going to get her hot sweaty little paws on one penny of his money. He'd worked hard for that house. It was his investment. He wasn't going to split the profits for it down the middle so that she could go and set up with her new toy-boy lover.

Let *him* buy his own house. Toy-boy could set her up in the style that she was always going on about.

Wooden floors. Hob cookers. Dishwashers!

He was welcome to her. She'd have him broke in no time!

Not that he'd let on to Alison that he didn't want a divorce. Barry smiled nastily.

He'd keep her dangling. It was the best way to keep women. On their toes.

Anyway he had Ciara and his

mother to think about, he thought self-righteously. He wouldn't upset them with a divorce. He had to be a *responsible* parent and son.

No! Divorce was not an option.

Barry scowled. If people didn't like it, they could bloody well lump it.

His life suited him just fine the way it was.

Chapter Seventeen

Six months later ...

"Assert yourself, Lillian. Assert yourself!" Lillian muttered fiercely. Her best friend, Mona Ryan, was always telling her to "assert" herself.

She saw Barry's car coming up the drive. Her heart fluttered. She felt as if telephones were dancing up and down her tummy.

In the hall stood four large black plastic sacks. She had packed his clothes, shoes, toothbrush and razor, papers and magazines into the four of them. Then she'd lugged them down the stairs.

She stood up and went to the sitting-room door. She was trembling.

Barry's key rattled in the door. He pushed it open.

"Hello," he muttered when he saw her.

Then he saw the bags.

"What's this?" He turned to her with a puzzled look on his face.

Lillian took a deep breath.

"It's time for you to go, Barry. When you came first, it was only for a few weeks. It's been over a year and you're still here. My life is not my own. Last Saturday, Mrs Ryan and I were watching a film and you came in and switched over to get the sports results. We missed the end of the film." Lillian's cheeks were bright pink but she carried on bravely.

"I won't have that any more. This is my house. I want to be able to entertain my friends. And I *don't* like sport," she said crossly.

"Oh! Sorry," grunted Barry.

"Anyway it's time you made up your mind what you're going to do with yourself. Either go back to your wife and child or go and live with that other one," Lillian ordered.

Barry said nothing. He lifted the black sacks out to the car, two by two. Minutes later he was gone.

Lillian couldn't believe it. It had been that easy. She'd asserted herself. Her life was her own again. She felt a million dollars. She took out the sherry bottle and two little glasses. She picked up the phone and dialled.

"Mona. He's gone. Come over and have a glass to celebrate. There's a good detective story on tonight. I'll make supper and we'll watch it in peace.

"Good woman yourself," Mona exclaimed. "I'll be over in a jiffy."

"*This is my happy day*," sang Lillian. "*This is the day that I'll remember the day I'm dying*." She hurried out to the kitchen to make a nice macaroni-cheese supper.

★

So it was decision time. Barry frowned. He could go back to Alison and Ciara or go and live with Brenda.

Neither choice enticed him. If he went home to Alison and Ciara he'd have to put up with Alison and her carry-on. If he went to live with Brenda, she'd nag him to get a divorce and marry her.

Barry stopped at the corner shop and got the *Evening Herald*. He thumbed through the property section. There were some nice little apartments around. One of them would suit him down to the ground. He wouldn't bother to tell Brenda that he'd left his mother's. He scanned the pages. There were several one-bedroom apartments advertised. He dialled the number of one on his mobile.

Two hours later, Barry stood in an egg-box-sized one-bedroom apartment overlooking the canal. It was perfect for him. Nice view. Hardly any housework, it was so small. A TV in the corner.

"I'll take it," he told the landlord.

What more could he want? He was a free man. No one would know that he had his own place. He unpacked his four black sacks. He washed his face, brushed his hair and rang Brenda.

"I'm coming over," he said. "I haven't eaten. I'll get us a bottle of wine. See you soon."

Brenda might be a nag but she was a great cook. He knew he'd get a decent dinner.

Barry smiled. A rare smile. He was happy.

★

Brenda flitted around the kitchen. She sliced and chopped and sprinkled and poured. A rich, tasty aroma filled the kitchen.

He had sounded in great form. He was bringing a bottle of wine. That was most unusual. Barry could be very mean, she'd discovered. He ate her out of house and home and took it for granted.

Maybe tonight was the night. Maybe at long last he was going to move in with her and ask her to marry him. Brenda ran upstairs and changed into a sexy low-cut top and a shorter skirt. She sprayed White Linen on her wrists. Her eyes danced with excitement.

Tonight was the night. It had to be. She'd put up with being a mistress for long enough.

★

"Are you sure you'll be all right?" Alison asked as she did a twirl around the bedroom. She was wearing a denim skirt and a belly top and she looked about sixteen. She had a great figure for a woman of her age, she told herself happily. She was off to Tomangos.

"I'll be fine," Ciara assured her. She had plans of her own.

She was inviting some of the girls from her new school over and they were going to order pizza and watch *Friends*. Everyone at school thought she was so lucky to have a free house every Friday and Saturday night. Her friends loved coming over. They thought Alison was cool. Ciara was very popular at her new school.

Some of them wanted to bring their boyfriends but Ciara said no. Girls only. Boys were not allowed. Boys turned into men and she knew better than anyone that men were horrible. Just like her father. She wanted nothing to do with men. They only made you unhappy.

It was a pity that Sara wasn't allowed to come. Kathy and Mike were very, very strict. Sara was always fighting with them because they wouldn't let her do things. It was awkward.

Ciara didn't stay with Kathy and Mike so much lately. She knew that they didn't approve of her being left alone in the house after school. And especially at night. They wouldn't let Sara stay unless there was an adult in the house.

It was silly. They weren't kids any more. They were at secondary school now.

Besides, Ciara liked being on her own. She could invite her new friends in to the house. They were cool. She liked being part of a gang.

Kathy and Mike had to let Sara grow up some time, Ciara told herself, as she applied eye shadow to her eyes and pale plum lipstick to her lips. She was a teenager. She was practically grown up.

Tomorrow night she and her friends were going to the pictures in the Omni. It was an over-sixteen but she'd get in easily. She'd done it before. And poor Sara would be stuck at home doing her homework.

Ciara felt very sorry for her former best friend.